Small Gifts

Stephen Evans

This is a work of creative non-fiction. Any events described in this book are true to the best of the author's recollection.

For Joan, who always noticed.

The contents of this book, with revisions, was previously published in *Layers of Life*.

Small Gifts: First Edition

ISBN: 978-1953725653

Time Being Media LLC

SMALL GIFTS

What these strong masters wrote at large in miles, I followed in small copy in my acre; For there's no rood has not a star above it.

Ralph Waldo Emerson

Society and Solitude

STEPHEN EVANS

Contents

Foreword

For Joan

Where are you now? I can only guess.
Surely where the purple-shifted light,
Powered by heart, marks the ancient way
To where the spirit generates each day,
Though here a twinkle only in the night,
In memory, in harmony, to bless.

STEPHEN EVANS

The Peaceful Place

I come here often.

About a quarter of a mile down the path behind my home, the trail curves and broadens into an asphalt circle. About 30 feet uphill from a tiny creek that wanders through the northern end of the park, the circle has three occupants: a woodenish bench, a large rock, and me.

I say woodenish because it looks like wood but feels like some sort of composite material, much harder than wood and I suppose more durable. It is painted a wood brown color and is comfortable enough for the occasional visitor like me.

The rock is about three feet by four feet, and maybe 18 inches high of some dark stone, sedimentary I think because it is formed in thin layers, shale perhaps, though flecks here and there glitter like diamonds. Maryland is home to a black shale deposit known as the Marcellus shale, which grew up about 400 million years ago when the state was a shallow sea. The rock has secrets, I can tell, maybe fossils hidden inside, but it is not telling, not me anyway.

It occurs to me that both rock and bench will be here long after me. They were here first, and so that seems fair.

The bench faces east and the sun warms my right cheek, while the breeze cools my left hand. There is little noise from cars, and only the occasional plane overhead. Surprising for a densely populated area, the ambient noise is mostly natural. I close my eyes to listen.

There's a wood dove behind me, a mockingbird up and to the right, a smaller sweet-voiced bird I can't identify somewhere in front. In the distance the brazen call of the crows disrupts the serenity from time to time. The trees in their buds rustle quietly now – their voices will grow with their leaves. The loudest sound is the crackle of squirrels as they chase though the dried leaves, until the hammering of a sapsucker opens my eyes.

I turn to locate him. The red headdress makes it easy. A tall slender tree has fallen across the creek, only to be caught partly upright by another tree on the opposite bank. The sapsucker is traversing the fallen tree looking for soft spots. The business of life goes on.

I always think of my father here. We used to stop here on our walks in his last year; a great walker most of his life, it was as far as he could go, or maybe as far as I thought he could. But he didn't mind stopping. I think it was peaceful for him too.

I have had other peaceful places.

This is the closest.

The others are far away in space or time or both.

Lake of the Isles was just down the block from our house in Minneapolis, and I absorbed its peace daily during the dissolution of my marriage. It was also gracious enough to inspire a story I have been writing for twenty years now.

Some of the peaceful others I have only visited once. Mallory Dock in Key West – though you wouldn't think to find peace in the middle of that circus atmosphere. It also inspired a story.

A pond in Pipestone Minnesota where wings of dragonflies conducted a symphony I could not hear.

A spot outside Devil's Tower, the quietest place I have ever been, where the deer and the antelope play.

Another south of Yellowstone where the white noise of waterfall enveloped me in solitude.

All these I have celebrated in books, and hope to celebrate in person once more in this life.

I can't remember any I had as a child. Perhaps it was just my bedroom, where I hid in my books. I was an inside child, asthma probably as formative in my growth as any factor. There was a tree in our backyard with a swing. Maybe that was one: I wrote a poem about it years later.

I hadn't realized before this how many of my peaceful places I have written about. They are important to me no doubt. I have a brain that is at best restless and at worst relentless. Imagining these places helps to calm me, to keep in check the unbounded notions I am prone to even now.

I hope everyone has a peaceful place, or more than one. We need them in this anxious world.

But if you don't, feel free to borrow one of mine.

I'll be the one smiling when you get there.

STEPHEN EVANS

No One Expects Metasequoia Glyptostroboides

I like trees.

I'm not exactly sure when this relationship began. But I think it might have been in 1970, on a family vacation to California. We flew out to San Francisco and drove down the coast to LA, stopping for a few days in Yosemite, where I took 1000 or so bad photos, which are now bad and unwatched slides. And somewhere around there we also saw Redwoods.

There were many of them, I think, but not a whole forest of them. And I'm not sure but I believe we saw one that you could drive through. I don't really remember how they looked, exactly, or what I thought. But I remember how they made me feel. I remember being surrounded by a sense of immense age, impressed with the realization that there were beings on this earth measured in frames outside the human.

That was nearly fifty years ago, a long time for me, a moment for them. For some reason over the last few years, I have felt a strong desire to see them again. I'm not sure why, or why now. Maybe I hope something so ancient will make me feel young again. Or maybe just a worry that they, along with so much else, may soon disappear, from erosion or drought or acid rain or who knows. Things disappear – I have learned that. But they also appear.

There is a path behind my house where I walk once or twice most weeks, for the last decade or so. The crooked tree is there, so is the straight one, and most of the others I have written about. I was walking a few days ago when I saw this one.

It's a redwood. Not a California Redwood, but a Dawn redwood, Metasequoia glyptostroboides, an Asian cousin. It won't grow as tall as Sequoia sempervirens or as large as Sequoiadendron giganteum. But it is a redwood. A beautiful one. And it had been there, a hundred yards from my home, for years.

So keep an eye out for redwoods. My new motto is: No one expects Metasequoia glyptostroboides.

Hope

Behind my home there is a young tree, a sapling I suppose, planted a few years ago to replace another that had died. It's a maple I think and this year was the first that the leaves turned that rich autumn red.

Most of them are gone now, fallen as is usual, but at the very top of the tree there is a cluster that hangs on. For some reason, every time I see them, they give me hope. I think we may have to rephrase Emily Dickinson a bit:

Hope is the tree with red leaves
That linger at the top
And waver in the winter wind
And never wish to drop

The Big Reveal

The leaves are fading fast now, falling in waves and beginning to shower the ground in brown.

The colors are dim this year, I suppose because the rain was limited. The connection between water and color is a mysterious one, an algorithm I cannot fathom, except to say that just enough, at just the right time, is a condition of brilliance.

But one thing I do appreciate about the leafless trees is the revelation of structure. I have long been fascinated by this, drawn to something elemental in the vision. I wonder why each tree happened to grow in that unique and complex way - what combination of water, wind, heredity and happenstance has led to this specific existential architecture.

My favorites are the trees at night, dark grey trunks and branches barely revealed against the deeper sky. On a clear night, the stars shine between the branches, as though the leaves have been reincarnated as celestial bodies.

Maybe that's what winter is for, to drop the veneer and let the heaven show through.

The Language of Trees

The trees were winking at me this morning. Or maybe it was morse code.

Tiny brights lights kept going on and off, as if someone was hitting a switch. But irregular, like a cipher.

I finally figured it out.

It was the light of the sun refracting through raindrops as the leaves moved in the breeze.

Nature speaks to us.

I hope we are listening.

STEPHEN EVANS

The Architecture of Trees

The architecture of trees fascinates me. How do the branches know how to grow?

Complexity theory?

Fibonacci Sequences?

Artificial intelligence?

A complex algorithm it must be.

In searching for its own light, the branch serves the tree. What does the branch know of the tree?

The result seems always the same:

Spare beauty against the blue.

STEPHEN EVANS

Tree Song

I don't know why the caged bird sings. But I think I may have finally figured out why the others do.

I take walks every day down a wooded path behind my home. Sometimes so many birds are singing it sounds like a choir. Other times there are only one or two at each turn of the path. Occasionally the songs sound like a dialogue, sometimes a Bach canon. But most often the sounds are clearly ecstatic, a brimming forth of some secret joy.

I believe I have discovered the source of that joy. Each bird is singing about how beautiful its tree is. How delicately shaped each leaf as it twists in the breeze. How the broad canvas of the whole creates ever evolving shadows on the ground. How the Fibonacci architecture of the branches leads right up to the sky.

Birds never sing about what time they have to get to the bird feeder, or whether they need a bath, or the bird next door, or even that tree they saw two weeks ago. They only sing of the beauty in front of them.

Each bird sings in its own language. Birds are very smart; each knows all the languages of all the birds. But when they sing of trees they sing in their own tongue, the one they hold in their heart.

And when they fly to the next tree, birds sing about how beautiful that tree is. And I agree with them.

I have never seen a tree that was not beautiful, from smallest sapling to startling senior. And unique – no tree the same as any other– even the aspen trees (which reproduce by what is called root sprouting and are in a sense one tree) are genetically identical but never quite the same in appearance. I wonder sometimes if the beauty of trees has something to do with their uniqueness—and if we were more aware of it in humankind, we might see more beauty in each other.

Do the trees listen to the birds? I think so. Do they appreciate the praise? I'm not so sure. The lives of trees seem unconcerned with birds, or squirrels, or humans. They have their own purposes in their long lives.

What beauty do trees sing about?

I doubt we will ever know.

The Leaf or the Shadow

I was taking a walk at noon or so, when a leaf fell from a tree a few feet in front of me. Even on the asphalt path,

I could see the darker shadow of the descending leaf, and I watched them both. The leaf as it fell twisted and turned, and lurched this way and that in the breeze, almost as though it were trying to escape the shadow below it. With each twist and lurch, the shape of the shadow altered, even though the leaf itself did not change shape. When it finally reached the ground and joined the waiting shadow, the shape of the leaf and shape of the shadow matched perfectly under the sun.

One of these is like life, I thought.

But is it the leaf?

Or the shadow?

Heard in a Dream

Go Figure

It is the steps that make the path.

Gratitude

Being grateful for the life you never planned takes planning.

A World Apart

The thing about living on a sphere is that as you are drifting apart you are also coming together.

Which Way

Is the snowflake facing?

Everything Lasts Forever

Just not all at once.

Nothing

When nothing can be done, nothing is everything.

The Trick

Imagine now as you wish to remember then.

Heard in a Dream

Do not open the silence. Let the silence open you.

Randomness

Seems unlikely.

Spin

Don't we all?

Is This Happiness?

What's missing in my life has been missing so long I don't miss it anymore.

Always

Tell the kindest truth.

Don't

Put on sunglasses before you leave the house. There is too much too beautiful to see.

Some

Some do not go gentle into that good night. Some know it is the night that they are leaving.

The Morning After Rain

The stream remembers.

Whence and Whither

The whence of beauty always is unclear. The whither, that we know, is far from here.

In the Time It Takes You

Time takes you.

The Summoning of Courage

Is the most dangerous of spells. For you cannot summon courage to do one thing. You must summon courage to do all things.

As a Rule

Rule of Life 1: do the most you can for the most you can.

Rule of Life 2: Include yourself in Rule 1.

People

Care about different things the same and the same things differently.

Grief

Is a response, not a process. We are the process.

I Wish

I could take a picture of what I see when my eyes are closed.

1,2,...

When I try to make every minute count, I end up just counting the minutes.

Kindness

An act of kindness is like a stone thrown into a great lake. The tiny waves move out until they cannot be seen, but always return again, though they may go unnoticed in stormy waters.

Sadness

Is like the ring of a tree. We grow around it but it is always there. And in the winter growth is slow.

The Universe Explained

It's not that the universe is expanding. It's that everything in it is shrinking, as we are siphoned off into Eternity.

It's Time

For the Timeless.

Some Mistakes

You make anyway.

Golf Wisdom

You always make the last putt.

The Key to Life

Is you don't need a key. The door is already open.

Taut

The lesson is the lesson.

Maybe

There would be more grace in the world if there were more grace in the world.

Reach for the Moon

If you miss, you end up in the cold dead vacuum of space. But it's beautiful out there and the moon's not much better really.

A Dream

I had a dream that when we die, the story of our life is added to the universe. A good life becomes light. A bad life becomes dark energy that sends the heavens spinning apart. So we decide our fate.

Beautiful Things

Recently, I subscribed to an app on my phone that is supposed to help with relaxation and meditation, using images of nature accompanied by peaceful music. Lots of flutes. I like to listen while I work; it cuts the silences of working from home.

I was reading one day, listening, glancing up occasionally to see what beautiful thing was on. Suddenly I felt sad, but I wasn't sure why. After a while, I realized that I was sad because I would never actually see the beautiful things that were on the screen. Except on a screen. I may never visit a beach in Thailand at sunset, or the Alps at sunrise. Because of time. Because of distance. Because of money. Because of age or health. It is world of beautiful things but our time here is short and for most of us our resources are limited.

And then I thought, yet here I am now seeing these things on television at least. That is seeing of a kind. Some of them I might have guessed at their existence. But many I would likely never have known about, except for this seeing. And if the images in this program are beautiful, there are many more beautiful images, stunning and extraordinary and strange, shown on TV and the Internet these days, on channels dedicated to them.

And not just natural beauty. Art is more accessible than ever before. Major museums are putting images of masterpieces within the reach of everyone at a click or two. And music also. Sites stream Bach and Mozart, Schubert and Prokofiev (my personal favorite), and so many more, many I have never heard of. Fifty years ago– no make that one hundred years ago, I forget how old I am–you would have had to attend a concert in Oslo or Vienna or New York to hear them.

This is a miraculous age of beautiful things, offered to us wherever we turn. I'm sure that they are more beautiful to experience in person. I would rather see them at a concert in Oslo, an evening at the

Met in New York, or flying over the Alps at sunrise (okay, I might have to close my eyes at that one).

But even in seeing them in this removed way, they are still beautiful. And I can see more of them this way than I could possibly see in a lifetime. That's a gift, and something to be grateful for.

The Price of Beauty

Something has devoured my flowers.

I suspect it was the deer.

A family of deer (buck, doe, and two fawns) have been coming to the parkish place behind my apartment for a couple of weeks. They are beautiful, and wild, and tame, and charming. They have no fear of humans, or their dogs, though if you approach they will grudgingly move on.

They come most often in the late afternoon, and I can see them as I sit writing. Sometimes I find them hiding from the sun under a large pine tree in the front, as I walk out to get the mail. The fawns are a few weeks old at most, and I can see their legs trembling still as they stand and munch the grass, or the leaves that have fallen during the frequent summer storms. I had planted the flower seeds sometime in June, in the 10x4 patch of ground that serves for a garden in front of my porch.

I don't recall what kind of flowers they were. I had ordered a packet of seeds for flowers that would attract butterflies. They had grown to about 8 to 10 inches tall, the largest with broad oval-shaped leaves, handsome and not at all delicate. They had not flowered, so I don't know what kind or color they would have been. And now I will never know.

When I woke this morning and looked out, all of the leaves had been eaten, leaving bare slender stalks standing like small green telephone poles, or an invasion of tiny slender aliens. Perhaps they will grow leaves again. But I doubt it.

I was angry at first – these are the first of anything that I had planted myself (though honestly I did little more than disturb the ground and sprinkle). And water faithfully, as instructed.

But now, I suppose I can't blame the deer; they have offered fair trade, beauty for beauty.

Perhaps beauty is the price of beauty, always a trade, beauty like energy being never created nor destroyed. The law of conservation of beauty.

And perhaps that applies to many areas of life, as well, all things in balance on the seesaw of eternity. Perhaps.

But until the deer start hovering delicately over my garden like butterflies, I will regret the loss of my flowers.

What If

I became a vegetarian not because it was more healthy or even more ethical, but because I did not want to add to the anguish in the world. I have never regretted that decision, or even seriously questioned it.

But what if everyone was a vegetarian? What if overnight some switch was thrown and no one ate meat any longer?

Sounds great, doesn't it? But I wonder what would happen to the billions of animals raised for food around the globe? Would they starve? Would we have massive euthanasia because we couldn't afford to feed them?

And suppose it was a gradual transition, no massive change, just fewer and fewer animals slaughtered. That would certainly mean fewer and fewer animals raised. Is it really better for them never to live than to live a while?

Take away the quality-of-life issues: if the life was comfortable and the death painless, which would be better—some life, or none? If you had to make that same choice for yourself, or your family, which would you choose?

Animals cannot choose the life we give them. But they can't choose the life we don't give them either.

Peace

I was sitting outside on my porch today reading for a few hours. All during that time birds came visiting.

First there was a beautiful jay, stunning blue and quiet for once, nestled into a spot in the sun just a few feet away.

Then a robin.

Then a few grosbeaks.

Some sparrows.

Dad's favorite wren who lives in the azalea next door.

A woodpecker on the nearby tree.

Others I couldn't name.

And now there is a doe settled in the shadowed grass about 100 feet away, testing the breeze, with a young buck standing close. Just living.

All just living.

Was that so hard, Life?

Layers of Life

Just outside my patio there is a large azalea bush. It blooms beautiful pink-orange blossoms for about two weeks each year, usually in May. The rest of the year it looks like most any large green bush.

I was sitting by the sliding glass doors that lead to the patio today and I noticed that there was a small swarm of gnats circling in chaotic patterns over the top of the bush. I had never noticed them before. Then I began to think of all the life associated with that one azalea bush.

There are the gnats, who seemed to find it for the moment entirely fascinating, and also a family of sparrows who make it their year-round home, along with a pair of wrens, and family (the baby who keeps trying to get into the apartment and makes me wonder if it is my Dad reincarnated because he loved wrens and loved to sing) and the cardinal pair who drop by for periodic visits along with the butterflies who arrive happily during that colorful two weeks, and disappointedly the rest of the year and the curious bees, especially the large bumblebees who find it intriguing along with the juncos, winter residents, and the wood doves, who love to sun themselves at the base of it next to the ants who make their homes in the soil and climb the wall beside it to get the larger view while beneath the soil, mixed in with the roots, who knows what denizens lurk—grubs and worms and for 16 and a half years, surely cicadas too, to say nothing of a teeming microbiome wholly unknown to me as I stare out.

Sorry—I've been reading Kerouac again.

Life is more than we know.

Attention is a path to joy.

STEPHEN EVANS

The Bug and the Blade

I was looking out my back window this Sunday morning and about ten feet away I noticed a bug climbing a blade of grass.

I shouldn't have been able to see something so small at that distance, but the blade was angled just so that the bug glinted like polished bronze in the sun. She struggled up that smooth green slippery surface until it bent down and was hidden.

And it struck me then how vast the world is, and how very very tiny is our part in it. And how many many stories come and go without notice. And how writers, the ones who notice and record, have an impossible and important job to do.

I waited to see if it would fling her into the air when she reached the end, but neither bug nor blade reappeared. Like Frosts' birches, it set her set her gently down again onto the earth, bent for the moment by her passing.

I kept watch a good while.

One could do worse than be a writer of notices.

Time to Sing

So there's this cricket.

He comes to visit every August, and he stays in the wall of my bedroom. His living room seems to be the window frame by my bed, I think because it is the best place to sing. It is long and slender, almost like an echo chamber.

He does like to sing.

Especially at night.

My hearing is pretty sensitive. And I find I am unable to fall asleep while he (or she – we've never actually met in person) is serenading me.

So if I have been a little grumpy lately, I apologize. I am not getting as much sleep as usual.

Not to be un-neighborly, but I have tried to convince him to move. I drop essential oils in a small hole in the window frame, which are supposedly too aromatic for the species. I shoot compressed air down the chamber, hoping to convince him a hurricane is approaching and he should take (other) shelter. I put in an ultrasonic device.

None of these have worked. But I refuse to take more drastic measures. I don't want to hurt him; I just want him to find another place to sing.

I have also tried ways to co-exist. Noise generators. Ear plugs. These help, but not enough.

I thought perhaps he might be insulted at the lengths I would go to avoid his song. If someone did that while I was singing, I think I would get the hint. But he keeps on singing, even knowing that he is singing to himself.

But it occurred to me this morning that we are the same in this way. He keeps on singing whether anyone is listening. I keep on writing whether anyone is reading.

I'm luckier than him. Once his song is done, it is gone. My words will last a bit. I can't say how long. But longer than I will, likely. And that is one of the things that keeps me writing.

He is singing now as I write this. And as I am singing in my own way here, I think: “keep singing little one”.

Everyone needs their time to sing.

Days of the Cicadas

There was a 1962 movie called Day of the Triffids, starring of all people Howard Keel, about an alien invasion. That is what it feels like around my home today. Brood X has arrived.

Brood X is the term for this brood of cicadas, which has lived underground for 17 years, to emerge for a short time to mate and lay eggs. There are billions of them all over the Mid and North Atlantic seaboard in the US. And my home seems to be Ground Zero.

A cicada, if you have never seen one, is (in this recent incarnation), a winged insect maybe an inch and a bit long. They are surprisingly gentle flyers, and most prefer to perch on the trunks of trees. Oak and beech so far seem to be the favorites as far as I have seen. The din that they make is loud and exotic, even otherworldly, as if stepping outside you have stepped through to a jungle, or another planet. These are the Days of the Cicadas.

I have been around long enough to have seen them before. I have memories of a high school baseball game, the tall wooden poles of the field lighting almost invisible under the covering horde. There are other broods, but this one is the largest by far.

Unlike other swarms, the cicadas do no harm, but harm comes to them. They are something of a feast for the local bird population. I have heard that they are edible by humans, but I have seldom been more thankful to be a vegetarian.

After they have mated, they descend to the ground, and wait patiently to die. This is what fascinates me about them. Seventeen years in the ground for a few moments in the light. I have yet to unpack the richness of this metaphor.

But something about them I find heroic. Maybe it is that at the end of their lives they find the energy to create. I root for them as I see them flying into the trees, rooting for myself in the process.

The Butterfly and the Bee

As we all know, I have a low threshold of fascination. Today for example as I have been working on a book, I have also been keeping an eye on my petunias. I have never had petunias before, so perhaps that accounts for some of the fascination. But really what garnered my attention for the last few hours is two visitors: a butterfly and a bee.

Initially actually I was watching a pail of water. It's very hot today and I had set out what I hoped would be a makeshift birdbath. As I watched the pail, the water looked still and undisturbed. But the bright sun threw a reflection of the water onto the roof of my porch. In the reflection I could see the water moving, from the wind or maybe convection currents as the water heated in the brutal daylight. The reflection also showed the rippling waves as my gift evaporated. I felt like I had my own little Plato's cave, except the reflection was truer than the actual. Though I suspect that was true of Plato's as well.

But then the butterfly appeared, a large one, likely a swallowtail (my older brother would know), black wings with blue and gold spots. She (I think) kept flying around the weeds in my little garden. I have weeds in my garden, a lot of them this year. I leave them there because I don't hurt anything if I don't have to and they seem to feel the same. Anyway, the butterfly kept landing on one after another of the weeds, continually disappointed I assume, and completely ignorant of the cornucopia of petunias in the hanging basket not five feet overhead. Every once in a while she would float up and I would think—there, now she's finally got it! But, so far at least, she has not made the leap. Perhaps it was an aesthetic choice and green is her preference. But the purple and pink treasure remained unclaimed. By the butterfly anyway.

The bee came later. A tiny one—though as scarce as bees have become around here I was glad to see any—found the petunias. But instead of gorging on the large full flowers, he instead insisted on trying to make his way into the nearly closed nearly dead blossoms, skipping entirely the glorious siblings. I watched him disappear into the narrow passage, and could see the from the turbulence outside the tunnel how difficult his passage was. I don't if he made all the way it in, nor what he found when he got there. Maybe he just wanted a challenge. Or maybe the ripened juice is sweeter. Perhaps the bee knew his business better than I.

There are many morals that could be drawn here. But I will leave it to you, and the butterfly, and the bee. My wish is simply this:

May you be fascinated by flowers.

STEPHEN EVANS

The Spider

A single strand of spider's web was strung across my porch this morning. I would never have seen it if the sun hadn't caught it just right. How in the world could one tiny spider have strung that slender thread, eight feet or more over open space?

Was he saying "See what I can do and you can't"?

Or was he saying "See what can be done"?

The truth is, he wasn't saying anything, has no knowledge of me, was just living his life in the world.

It's not all about me. I keep forgetting
that.

But see what can be done.

I keep forgetting that too.

The Butterfly on the Blossom

We had a guest today.

A butterfly stopped by the azalea outside my window. I was able to get a quick photo. Then he was gone.

After he left, it occurred to me that I didn't feel regret that he was gone. I felt grateful that he had stopped by, that I was there at that moment to see that fleeting convergence.

I find it hard sometimes to recognize the small gifts. But I'm getting better at it. I notice the birds singing more often these days. I'll stop and admire a tree. Or clouds. Or grass. The brilliance of the green in sunlight. Or sunlight, half an hour before sunset when the angle of the light makes everything crystal.

What I have difficulty with, always, is regretting. I don't let things go. People. I don't let people go, even when they have been gone a long time.

Still.

The butterfly is on the blossom.

Rejoice. And be glad.

Thinking Small

When I go for a walk, I often have my head down. So far I haven't bumped into anyone. Or they haven't bumped into me. I suppose social distancing has helped, when it comes to that.

I like to think that other sojourners imagine I am deep in thought pondering vast questions of human existence. More likely, they think I am anti-social, which I suppose is partly true.

The real reason I look down as I walk is so I don't step on anyone (or more than one). I am convinced that after death, if there is a tribunal with

St. Peter or Rhadamanthus or Anubis, the primary category of judging will be how many beings you have stepped on (or otherwise hurt) and how many saved. And I don't think size matters—a being is a being in my ecosystemic view. Maybe you even get credit for thinking small.

I believe I am doing well in the Karma department, though I don't have an actual count to offer. Though I'm hoping that beings I can't see don't count, or better that I don't hurt them if I do step on them. There is more biomass in bacteria than in any other form of animal life, so that worries me a bit.

All in all, it makes for a gentle life, seeking goodness where it exists, beauty where it is found, laughter as it comes, and joy in everything. Thinking small makes you a small part of a larger life, instead of a large part of a smaller one.

It's worth the tradeoff.

STEPHEN EVANS

Acknowledgements

Many of these pieces have appeared on The Green Room at:

https://www.gr8word.com

STEPHEN EVANS

About the Author

Stephen Evans is a playwright and the author of *The Island of Always, Whose Beauty is Past Change, A Transcendental Journey, Funny Thing Is: A Guide to understanding Comedy,* Find him online at:

https://www.istephenevans.com/

STEPHEN EVANS

Books by Stephen Evans

Fiction:

The Island of Always:
The Marriage of True Minds
Let Me Count the Ways
My Winter World
The Marriage Gift
Paradox
Whose Beauty is Past Change
The Mind of a Writer and other Fables
Epigrammaticon
The Next Joy and the Next

Non-Fiction:

Funny Thing Is: A Guide to Understanding Comedy
Prolegomena to Any Future Vacation
Layers of Life
Liebestraum
The Laughing String: Thoughts on Writing

Plays:

The Visitation Quartet:

The Ghost Writer

Monuments

Tourists

Spooky Action at a Distance

At the Still Point

Experience	*Three plays about Ralph Waldo Emerson*
Generations	*(with Morey Norkin and Michael Gilles)*
As You Like It	*(by William Shakespeare, adapted by Stephen Evans)*
The Glass Door	*(An adaptation of Hedda Gabler by Henrik Ibsen)*

STEPHEN EVANS

Verse:

Limerosity
Limerositus
Sonets from the Chesapeke
The Crooked Mirror

STEPHEN EVANS

www.ingramcontent.com/pod-product-compliance
Lightning Source LLC
Chambersburg PA
CBHW030905200726
48289CB00003B/900